# Internet Governance
# in an Age of Cyber Insecurity

D1553408

**COUNCIL** *on*
**FOREIGN**
**RELATIONS**

*International Institutions and*
*Global Governance Program*

Council Special Report No. 56
September 2010

Robert K. Knake

# Internet Governance in an Age of Cyber Insecurity

**Mixed Sources**
Product group from well-managed
forests and other controlled sources
www.fsc.org   Cert no. SW-COC-001530
© 1996 Forest Stewardship Council
FSC

# Contents

# Foreword

The Internet, since its debut in 1989, has revolutionized commerce, communication, military action, and governance. Much of the modern world is simply inconceivable without it. This revolution, however, has not come without a price. The annual cost of cyber crime has now climbed to more than $1 trillion, while coordinated cyberattacks have crippled Estonia, Georgia, and Kyrgyzstan and compromised critical infrastructure in countries around the world. While no fewer than six UN bodies and multiple regional and national forums have sought to build a consensus on the future of Internet governance, there has been little progress thus far. The United States has largely abstained from these discussions, instead focusing on developing its own offensive and defensive cybersecurity capabilities while entrusting the ongoing stability of the system to the expertise of the private sector.

In this Council Special Report, Robert K. Knake briefly examines the technological decisions that have enabled both the Internet's spectacular success and its troubling vulnerability to attack. Arguing that the United States can no longer cede the initiative on cyber issues to countries that do not share its interests, he outlines an agenda that the United States can pursue in concert with its allies on the international stage. This agenda, addressing cyber warfare, cyber crime, and state-sponsored espionage, should, he writes, be pursued through both technological and legal means. He urges first that the United States empower experts to confront the fundamental security issues at the heart of the Internet's design. Then he sketches the legal tools necessary to address both cyber crime and state-sponsored activities, including national prohibitions of cyber crime, multilateral mechanisms to prevent and prosecute cyberattacks, and peacetime norms protecting critical civilian systems, before describing the bureaucratic reforms the United States should make to implement effectively these changes.

*Internet Governance in an Age of Cyber Insecurity* is a timely contribution on an issue increasingly capturing the attention of policymakers. It presents technical ideas to the nonexpert in accessible and compelling language. The report leaves little doubt about the importance of cybersecurity to the future of both the United States and the Internet itself, and its recommendations provide a strong foundation for future action.

**Richard N. Haass**
*President*
Council on Foreign Relations
September 2010

# Acknowledgments

I could not have developed this report without the expertise, advice, and patience of the report's advisory committee. Each member of the committee possesses a far greater degree of expertise on these issues than I brought to this project and I am grateful for their willingness to share it and to struggle through innumerable drafts. Any remaining errors of fact or logic are my own.

Esther Dyson did an admirable job of chairing the advisory committee meetings while also lending her keen editorial eye and decades of experience within the Internet governance community. I am grateful to CFR President Richard N. Haass and to the CFR International Affairs Fellowship committee for giving me the opportunity to spend a year working on cybersecurity policy, and to Senior Vice President, Director of Studies, and Maurice R. Greenberg Chair James M. Lindsay for lending his support to make this project a reality and for patiently reviewing numerous drafts until the language was clear and the national interests of the United States well defined.

CFR's corporate and congressional programs provided me with the opportunity to test the ideas contained in this report in front of expert audiences prior to publication, and the report is much improved because of the feedback received from each session. James Lewis at the Center for Strategic and International Studies invited me to participate in meetings with the China Institute of Contemporary International Relations, where I gained an invaluable firsthand understanding of that country's goals and objectives for Internet governance.

I wish to thank John Rollins at the Congressional Research Service for helping me to understand the role of Congress in Internet governance and Vince Crisler at Zeichner Risk Analytics, LLC, for providing both valuable insight into the policy challenges and much-needed technical advice on the inner workings of the Internet. I am also grateful to Rod Beckstrom, president of the Internet Corporation for Assigned Names and Numbers (ICANN), who joined our first advisory committee meeting and shared his perspective. CFR Senior Fellow Adam Segal was a constant sounding board and took the time to help me reorganize the final draft and focus in on what U.S. national interests are in cyberspace and how best to pursue them.

Research Associate Preeti Bhattacharji kept the project on track and me on deadline, flawlessly handling every detail. Communications Coordinator Lucy Dunderdale helped shepherd me through the approval process for the report and did so cheerfully. Former CFR intern Rachel Harris provided research assistance, gracefully tackling a number of difficult requests on esoteric topics.

This report was developed under the auspices of the International Institutions and Global Governance (IIGG) program, led by Senior Fellow Stewart M. Patrick, who provided invaluable guidance on both content and structure. The project was made possible through a generous grant from the Robina Foundation.

**Robert K. Knake**

*Council Special Report*

# Introduction

The United States is being outmaneuvered in the international forums that will determine the future of the Internet. Led by Russia and China, nondemocratic regimes are organizing into a united front to promote a vision of the Internet that is tightly controlled by states. That vision is increasingly attractive to many Western nations wrestling with inter-related threats of cyber crime, industrial espionage, and cyber warfare. The United States must actively combat these threats while it works to protect U.S. national interests in the preservation and extension of the Internet as a platform for increased efficiency and economic exchange. Protecting this interest requires far more extensive engagement within Internet governance forums to shape the future of the network in a way that addresses security concerns without resulting in a cure that is worse than the disease.

In pursuit of this objective, the United States should be guided by three principles. First, it should take a networked and distributed approach to a networked and distributed problem. No single forum can adequately address this set of issues. Instead, it needs to nurture solutions through wide engagement across a broad set of forums. Second, the United States should move toward holding states accountable for their actions and those of their citizens and systems in cyber-space. Though the United States cannot expect countries to prevent all malicious behavior, it can expect them to secure their networks to a reasonable standard, pass laws outlawing international cyber crime, and have mechanisms in place to act on requests for assistance in shutting down attacks, and investigating and prosecuting them. Third, the United States should lead by example. It should take steps to clean up its national network, work to stop its systems from being used in international cyberattacks, prioritize criminal investigation of cyber-attacks with foreign victims, and make clear that the primary goal of its military efforts in cyberspace is to defend the United States and pre-serve international connectivity.

These principles should be applied to a three-part agenda. The United States should work to develop a stronger set of international regimes to fight crime in cyberspace, moving beyond the current Council of Europe Convention to draw in non-Western states, and develop real-time mechanisms for collaborating to stop cyberattacks in progress and investigate attacks across borders. Addressing cyber crime alone, how-ever, will not secure cyberspace. State actors should also be constrained through the development of new norms. The United States should not fear talks on these issues and should pursue treaties to protect the core functions of the Internet and ban distributed denial-of-service attacks. It should also reinvigorate efforts to secure the Internet's underlying technologies, which were developed decades ago for a different purpose than they are being used for today.

Finally, the United States should establish the mechanisms within its own government to pursue these agendas. Stronger White House leadership is necessary to keep the agencies with interests in how the Internet is developed focused on U.S. national interests. The issue of Internet governance within the State Department should be elevated to a new bureau focused on cyber affairs, and that bureau should be given the mission of working to improve security of cyberspace through inter-national engagement. The private sector should also be given a stronger voice on these issues and mechanisms developed for companies to both shape U.S. policy and coordinate their own positions.

# Background

Since the early days of the Internet, its main architects and supporters have sought to limit the role of governments in the network's design, operation, and governance. While the Internet is the product of decades of U.S. government–funded research, the computer scientists who developed the protocols that today's network runs on designed them so that no central operator of the network would be necessary. Throughout the past three decades, successive presidential administrations have consistently taken a hands-off approach to the development of the network to allow the Internet to grow without government involvement that could have limited or stalled its dramatic expansion. This approach has been extended into the international arena, where the United States has maintained control of the one necessary component of the Internet's underlying architecture that must be actively managed—the Domain Name System (DNS)—but has otherwise taken the position that the role of governments in managing the network should remain limited. The rise of cyber crime, the emergence of cyber espionage, and the specter of cyber warfare have led many foreign governments to exert sovereign authority over their networks and to press international organizations to take up these issues.

## UNDERSTANDING THE THREAT

Cyber crime damage to the global economy is estimated at more than $1 trillion each year.[1] Sophisticated attacks targeting intellectual property of Fortune 500 companies are becoming routine. State actors are entering the mix, developing both offensive and defensive capabilities in a new form of arms racing. The United States is in the process of starting up Cyber Command, a new combatant command charged with both offensive and defensive operations in cyberspace that will be headed by a four-star general. At least four other countries have developed advanced offensive cyber operations capabilities and more than one hundred have begun to organize cyber warfare units.[2]

These capabilities have not been confined to the lab. In 2007, Estonia suffered a national-level denial-of-service attack that took the entire nation offline for a week, affecting government, telecommunication, and financial networks.[3] A year later, when Russia invaded Georgia, the ground and air forces were preceded by an onslaught in cyberspace. These early conflicts in cyberspace are likely harbingers of far worse attacks. Researchers have demonstrated the capability to use cyberattacks to destroy financial records, turn off the power, and disrupt networks necessary for military operations. Critical infrastructure sectors—including power, oil and gas, and water and sewer—are increasingly targeted.[4]

## INTERNET GOVERNANCE TODAY

As a network of networks, the Internet has no central authority to control it.[5] New technical standards for the protocols that make the Internet function are developed through an iterative "request for comment" process managed by the Internet Engineering Task Force (IETF) and adopted by the technical community on a consensus basis. Recognizing the need for a centralized authority to assign unique name and number identifiers, the Domain Name System was developed in the early 1980s. The role of allocating IP addresses and managing the root zone (the names and IP addresses of the authoritative DNS servers for all top-level domains such as .com) was handled by a single individual, Jon Postel, for almost two decades.[6] In 1998, the U.S. Department of Commerce created the Internet Corporation for Assigned Names and Numbers to oversee the management of this system of unique identifiers.

ICANN operates the only centralized system necessary to keep the Internet functioning. ICANN fulfills this important role at minimal cost and is taking measures to address security issues within its mandate. Many Internet pioneers and supporters of Internet freedom maintain that the assignment of these unique identifiers is the only necessary Internet governance function. Successive U.S. administrations have largely agreed, limiting U.S. government involvement and seeking to keep other governments from attempting to exert authority over the network in order to allow it to grow unencumbered. The rising tide of malware, rampant identity theft, financial crime, terrorist use of the Internet, unprecedented levels of corporate espionage, and the development of offensive cyber warfare and cyber exploitation capabilities by state actors, however, suggests that stronger and more expansive governance may be necessary for the Internet to grow and continue to add value to global commerce and enrich the daily lives of billions.

Given the costs of crime, the economic threat of industrial espionage, and the increasing militarization of cyberspace, the laissez-faire approach that the United States has taken toward Internet governance over the past decade can no longer be sustained. Though today's Internet is the product of a collaborative effort by the U.S. government, private sector, and academic community, historical bragging rights do not translate into control of the Internet's future. If the United States fails to provide the leadership necessary to address the security problems, other states will step in. If the current Internet is a reflection of the openness and innovation that are hallmarks of American society, the Internet of the future envisioned by Russia and China would reflect their societies—closed, dysfunctional, state-controlled, and under heavy surveillance.

## NEW INTERGOVERNMENTAL INITIATIVES

Given the security concerns, many countries are pressing new initiatives to secure cyberspace in a dizzying number of international forums that are now vying for a role in Internet governance, including at least half a dozen entities within the United Nations alone. Regional groups—including the Asia-Pacific Economic Cooperation (APEC) forum, the Organization for Economic Cooperation and Development (OECD), and the Organization of American States (OAS)—are also active. The Russian government has been pushing since 1998 for a UN treaty to address conflict in cyberspace. Recently, however, the idea has begun to gain momentum. The concept received support at the Twelfth United Nations Congress on Crime Prevention and Criminal Justice in Salvador, Brazil, in April 2010.[7] Hamadoun I. Touré, the secretary-general of the International Telecommunication Union (ITU), is actively pursuing such a treaty and recently called for a UN conference that would define a "blue print for a system-wide approach" to cybersecurity.[8]

Such an outcome is clearly counter to U.S. interests. As an organization, the ITU is not designed to manage an issue as complex as cybersecurity and has no mandate to address issues of crime or interstate conflict. As a state-centric, intergovernmental organization, the ITU is also not set up for nongovernmental organizations and the private sector to participate in the discussion. Countering the momentum behind this initiative will require more than just ignoring it or arguing against it. Moving beyond the ICANN functions, the United States must work cooperatively with other countries to develop a better mechanism for international coordination to combat cyber crime, develop norms for warfare in cyberspace, and promote the development of a new, secure suite of Internet protocols.

# Rethinking U.S. Interests in Cyberspace

The United States' overriding national interest in cyberspace is to preserve and extend the Internet as a tool for economic efficiency at home and as a facilitator for economic exchange internationally. The current level of criminal activity, espionage, and preparation of the battlefield in cyberspace threatens to stall if not wipe out the economic gains produced by the networking of systems over the past two decades. Moreover, an overreaction to these threats could be equally devastating. In seeking to improve security in cyberspace, the United States must work to preserve the core attributes of the network that make it so valuable for economic exchange: innovation, openness, and limited governance. These attributes make the network flexible, so that new uses can be developed rapidly, and scalable, so that millions of new users and devices can be connected each year, expanding the free flow of ideas and the reach of international commerce. Addressing problems of security in cyberspace at the expense of these attributes would not serve U.S. national interests.

The tremendous gains in economic productivity over the past two decades are the direct result of the expanded use of the Internet for communication, collaboration, outsourcing, just-in-time inventory management, and the control of industrial processes. Internationally, the surge in global trade in both goods and services that has taken place could not have happened without the Internet as an enabling technology. Malicious activity in cyberspace threatens these systems. In the area of corporate espionage alone, many companies are beginning to question the wisdom of using the Internet to allow around-the-clock research and development across time zones due to the loss of intellectual property from attacks.

As the most wired nation in the world, the United States is also the most vulnerable to disruptive activity in cyberspace, be it threats to the system itself or threats carried on the system against networked targets.

Despite these vulnerabilities, the Obama administration is moving forward with plans that would increase, not decrease, U.S. dependency on networked technologies for the conduct of commerce, the control of critical systems, and the execution of government responsibility. The National Broadband Plan identifies expanded broadband access as the "foundation for economic growth, job creation, global competitiveness and a better way of life."[9] The plan identifies six "Goals for a High-Performance America," in which Internet systems would provide massive new efficiency gains in every economic sector and in the daily lives of each and every American. Goals include a national broadband network for first responders to provide interoperable communication during disasters and a Smart Grid that connects individual consumers to the power grid for real-time power usage and rate monitoring. Given the current cyber threat environment, extending U.S. dependence is at best naive and at worst could create a situation in which America's homeland is vulnerable to both state and nonstate actors that will seek to skip the battlefield and do harm to U.S. society in cyberspace.

In seeking to reduce these threats, the United States must also be mindful that security is not an end in itself, but a facilitator for economic exchange and improved efficiency. Too much security will reduce the usability of the network, slowing traffic and creating barriers for new uses and new users. While stronger governance is necessary, that governance should be tailored to specifically address a narrow set of security concerns surrounding crime and warfare. Proposals by China, Russia, and other authoritarian regimes to improve "information security"— their chosen phrase—are not in fact about these concerns, but about their desire to limit dissent and access to information deemed threatening to their regimes. Proposals to build in tracking to all packets so that every action taken on the network can be instantaneously traced back to an individual, for instance, would be cumbersome and costly and do little to combat crime or limit warfare. They would, however, constrain the average user's ability to access information and engage in political dialogue anonymously. Criminal groups, intelligence agencies, and militaries will find ways around such controls, while average users will be subject to near-total surveillance of their online activity.[10] Such a system would have a stifling effect on the usability of the network as well as harm U.S. interests in the promotion of freedom and democracy around the globe. Though there is little that the United States can do to convince China, Russia, and other authoritarian regimes that unrestricted Internet access and the openness and freedom of expression that come with it are in their national interests, the international community would be done a disservice if the global Internet evolved to reflect the values of these societies.

To avoid this outcome while preserving and extending the Internet as a mechanism for economic exchange and efficiency, the United States must work within the international system to constrain actors with malicious intent, develop cooperative mechanisms to pursue cyber criminals, limit espionage, and develop norms against the initiation of conflict in cyberspace. The alternatives to this approach are unappealing. They include being forced to scale back the networking of systems, extensive regulation for security that would be costly and burdensome, the active protection of critical infrastructure in cyberspace by government agencies similar to the takeover of airline security after 9/11, and the increased use of offensive capabilities to stop attacks. If the United States does not engage, other countries will shape the future of the Internet but undermine the network as a mechanism for the free exchange of information and political discourse. Clearly, in light of these alternatives, international engagement to improve security and limit action in cyberspace is preferable.

# Principles for Engagement

The United States is no longer the sine qua non for Internet governance. Nonparticipation within Internet governance forums by the United States will not keep other countries with objectives counter to those of the United States from shaping the future of the Internet. The United States gains nothing from being perceived as determined to use computer network attacks without limit. While it should focus most of its effort on building informal consensus and developing international mechanisms for cooperation, the United States needs to engage on its own terms rather than try to prevent international discussion of the topic. It has little to lose by talking.

As a general principle, the United States should support processes that allow representatives from the technical community, the private sector, and user and consumer groups to shape policy and avoid state-centric processes for handling technical issues. Intergovernmental forums, however, are necessary for bringing the rule of law to the Internet. Through engagement, the United States can shape solutions to the security challenges in cyberspace in ways that align with other interests in expanding international trade and achieving greater economic efficiency. The United States will need to develop separate agendas and strategies for pursuing these agendas in the areas of crime, limiting state actors, and developing secure standards, but there is a set of overarching principles that should broadly guide U.S. engagement in this area.

## TAKE A NETWORKED AND DISTRIBUTED APPROACH

To pursue its national interests in cyberspace, the United States should support open processes that welcome a wide range of participants from the technical community, the private sector, and user and consumer groups to shape policy and avoid state-centric processes for handling technical issues. No single forum can possibly encompass all the issues and players involved in addressing security concerns in cyberspace. Instead, the United States should nurture a range of forums—some multilateral, some bilateral, and some regional—to tackle these challenges. Separate coalitions may be necessary to address the technical agenda and various aspects of the international legal agenda, including crime, corporate espionage, and state conflict. Regional coalitions may also prove effective. Though cyber threats do not vary significantly by region, it may be easier to foster a series of agreements within regional organizations than to reach a global agreement. Instead of trying to cajole former colonies into a treaty put together by former colonial powers, replicating the Council of Europe Convention on Cybercrime in the Organization of American States, the African Union, and the Association of Southeast Asian Nations (ASEAN) may be more effective. Global coalitions that address more specific problems may also be effective. Initially, these coalitions should be loose and informal, seeking support from nations whose interests are aligned with those of the United States. Traditional U.S. allies are a good starting point, but efforts should be made to actively recruit more than the usual handful of Western suspects. A target list of nations from which to seek support could include the thirty-one countries in the OECD, plus smaller and less developed nations that are working to address cyber crime, including Estonia, the Philippines, and the Dominican Republic.

## HOLD STATES ACCOUNTABLE
## FOR THEIR ACTIONS

Security strategists have been paralyzed by the "attribution problem" for more than a decade. Attribution for cyberattacks is made difficult by four factors: first, cyberattacks do not require geographic proximity; second, there is no equivalent to radar systems to detect the origin of an attack as there was with Cold War missiles; third, the protocols that govern Internet traffic are fundamentally insecure and the origin of packets can be masked; and fourth, cyberattackers will typically use one or more compromised systems as the launching point for their attack, crossing multiple international boundaries in order to complicate the investigation process.

While technical solutions to the attribution problem and other security problems with the Internet's architecture must be pursued, the problem of attribution should not be overstated. At present, the ability to wage anything that rises to the level of "war" in cyberspace is possessed by at most twenty groups worldwide, half of which are nation-state actors and the other half of which are private criminal groups closely aligned with nation-states. In the event of a major attack, the list of potential suspects will be small. Technical means of identifying attackers continue to improve, but the importance of real-world intelligence and investigation should not be overlooked. Ironclad attribution by technical means may never be achieved, as criminals and cyber warriors will work to identify vulnerabilities in any new protocols or surveillance systems, though something akin to probable cause for further investigation can almost always be achieved.

When cyberattacks occur, all too often states will claim no responsibility and offer "patriotic hackers" who cannot be identified or controlled as the likely culprits. They will also refuse to allow investigators access to potential suspects or to systems involved in the incident on the grounds that doing so would violate national sovereignty. On at least two occasions—the attacks on Estonia and Georgia—this was the Russian response. Similarly, the Chinese government has cast off all responsibility for cyberattacks that originate from systems within its country. In early 2010, Google was able to trace a successful hacking campaign that stole proprietary information from Google and up to thirty other American companies back to servers in China. Chinese government officials argued that the systems used in the attacks were proxies that had been compromised due to the widespread use of pirated software and unsecure systems in their country. Each of these explanations may be true, but in either example, with evidence pointing toward criminal activity targeting one country that can be traced to another, the burden of proof should now shift to the country hosting the unlawful activity. Countries that do not cooperate in criminal investigations should understand that failure to cooperate will be treated as a sign of complicity. States can be held accountable for their actions, those of their citizens, and systems in cyberspace.[11] The United States requires a range of options and mechanisms for punishing states that routinely attack others in cyberspace or allow their territory or systems to be used by criminal groups. Responses can include both traditional diplomatic protest, sanctions, and military action as well as network actions, including higher-level scrutiny for Internet traffic leaving states that do not cooperate and ultimately blockading access to U.S. and allied networks from states that continue to be outliers.

## LEAD BY EXAMPLE

The United States cannot call on others to take action without also committing to show restraint in the use of force in cyberspace, curb cyber criminals at home, and take steps to reduce malicious activity on U.S. networks. Diplomatic efforts should make clear that U.S. military and intelligence activity in cyberspace is focused on defending the United States and protecting freedom of international information flows. The United States should commit to vigorously pursue criminal prosecution of any citizen that engages in "hactivism" against foreign states, and should expect other countries to do the same. On cyber crime, the Federal Bureau of Investigation (FBI) should be funded to dedicate resources to investigating cyber criminal activity that originates on U.S. soil but targets victims overseas. The United States should also lead efforts to clean up its portion of cyberspace, reducing its share of computers on the network that are either parts of botnets—networks of compromised computers used to carry out attacks—or the origination points for attacks. It should also work to establish mechanisms to shut down attacks on foreign systems that originate from U.S. systems in real time.

# Pursuing International Engagement

Guided by this set of principles, the United States should pursue its interests on three tracks. First, it should lead the creation of a stronger set of international regimes to fight crime in cyberspace. Because addressing cyber crime alone will not reduce threats to the network and to the network system to a sufficient level that they can be trusted, the United States must also pursue a second track to constrain state actors in cyberspace. Finally, the United States should undertake efforts to secure the Internet's underlying technologies.

## REDUCING THE THREAT OF CYBER CRIME

Cyber crime has become the occupation of choice for smart criminals because it offers low risks and high rewards. Whereas national legal authority is bounded by borders, the Internet is not. Criminals exploit this fact by carrying out cyber crime in one country from the safe confines of another, preferably one with weak laws and limited enforcement, investigation, or prosecutorial capabilities. Combating cyber crime, therefore, requires all countries to pass laws that make international cyber crime illegal, and to develop mechanisms to stop, investigate, and prosecute attacks originating in one country that target victims in another. The United States needs to put its weight behind multilateral initiatives that provide countries with assistance in developing legal frameworks and enforcement capabilities, a mechanism for judging the effectiveness of national efforts at combating cyber crime, and a process that provides both positive and negative incentives that promote adherence to international legal standards.

## FOCUS EFFORTS OUTSIDE THE COUNCIL OF EUROPE CONVENTION ON CYBERCRIME

Efforts to develop a solution to the problem of international cyber crime have centered on the Council of Europe's Convention on Cybercrime. The convention was developed to establish a baseline set of laws that parties to the treaty would pass to criminalize computer crimes and to provide a mechanism for cross-border cooperation.[12] The United States put its diplomatic weight behind the convention in 2000 after the failed prosecution of the author of the "ILOVEYOU" computer virus. In that incident, U.S. law enforcement authorities were able to trace the virus's development to a student group in the Philippines but were unable to gain extradition for the virus's author because the crime he had committed was not against Philippine law. The convention was finalized in November 2001 and came into force in July 2004 after five countries ratified it. As of May 2010, twenty-nine countries have ratified the treaty and seventeen signatories are in the process of considering ratification.[13]

Though the convention has helped develop an international standard for criminalizing cyber crime, it has not led to an appreciable reduction in cyber crime. The mechanisms for international cooperation developed by the convention are bilateral and prosecutorial, providing no conduits to coordinate law enforcement activity across borders or for network security professionals to coordinate technical solutions when attacks occur. Members of the convention include some of the worst cyber-criminal havens in eastern Europe, such as Romania and Bulgaria. Many countries, most notably Japan, have been unwilling to ratify the treaty simply because it was constituted under the Council of Europe. The convention has served a purpose in laying out a legal framework for harmonizing national laws on cyber crime and for providing cross-border mutual assistance, but adding signatories to this particular document is neither necessary nor sufficient for reducing cross-border cyber criminal activity. Unlike arms limitation treaties, where reductions by one state can occur only if all parties agree to a reduction in force, the passage of cyber criminal laws is in the interest of individual states regardless of whether other states pass such laws, because cyber criminals tend not to confine their activities solely to foreign targets.

## USE THE FINANCIAL ACTION TASK FORCE AS A MODEL

Though as a general rule, the United States should foster processes that are decentralized and inclusive of the technical community, the private sector, and user and consumer groups, there are certain problems only states can address. One of these is cyber crime. In creating a new regime to reduce international cyber crime, the goal should be to narrowly address existing problems in the investigation, apprehension, and prosecution of cyber criminals, with the lightest organization possible. In areas in which governments are the only actors with the authority to address problems in cyberspace, they should do so to the minimal extent possible.

The United States should therefore promote the adoption of national-level criminal laws and the development of less formal mechanisms for cross-border investigation and prosecution through the creation of a new intergovernmental body modeled on the Financial Action Task Force (FATF), an organization created to promote the development of national and international policies and capabilities to combat terrorist financing and money laundering.[14] Established in 1989 by the Group of Seven (G7) in concert with the European Commission and eight other countries, FATF began its work by establishing a set of forty recommended policies that countries should adopt. FATF quickly expanded, and now covers thirty-four countries that together account for most global financial transactions. After the terrorist attacks of September 11, 2001, combating terrorist financing was added to the FATF mission and the organization's standards were revised to address the new issue. In addition to developing recommended policies and standards, FATF also monitors member compliance with those standards and helps implement them. Monitoring is done on a multilateral peer-review basis under a program known as Mutual Evaluation. FATF has also given rise to a series of FATF-style regional bodies that have adopted a similar mission within specific geographic regions.[15] With an accepted set of standards and objective mechanisms for monitoring compliance, the FATF has created the basis upon which the United States and other countries can threaten noncompliant nations with the loss of access to international financial networks.

A similar organization should be established to do for cyber crime what FATF has done for money laundering. The United States— together with other OECD countries and smaller nations supportive of the agenda—should establish the organization and develop criteria to evaluate membership applications by other countries. The organization should begin by developing model policies based on the Council of Europe Convention, the ITU Toolkit for Cybercrime Legislation, and other recognized best practices.[16] As with the FATF, this work should be completed within the first year of the organization's existence. Once the recommended policies have been developed, the organization should begin assessing member countries against the developed standards. The assessments should also provide a roadmap for correcting any problems identified and establish a process for periodic review of progress made in addressing the identified problems.

### NAME, SHAME, AND SANCTION
### CYBER CRIMINAL SANCTUARIES

The organization should also conduct an annual global review of both member and nonmember countries that assesses countries' legal frameworks, enforcement capabilities, and overall levels of cyber crime. For other transnational problems, compiling an annual index or report of the best and worst states based on objective metrics has prompted many states to improve their behavior. Models include Transparency International's Corruption Index, the UN Office on Drugs and Crime World Drug Report, and the World Bank's Governance Matters Index. Oxford Internet Institute's Mapping and Measuring Cybercrime Forum has begun to explore what metrics could be used in such a ranking.[17] These rankings would be an effective mechanism for "naming and shaming" countries to address cyber criminal activity and to become members of the new organization.

These independent ratings could then be used as the basis for the organization to work with the worst states to develop plans to remedy the gaps in their legal and enforcement mechanisms. Ultimately, as with the FATF recommendations and evaluations, this process could provide the basis on which countries are sanctioned for failing to address cyber criminal activity. Sanctions could be undertaken bilaterally or multilaterally, and could include the withholding of development dollars targeted for Internet infrastructure development. Countries that do not clean up their cyberspace could have their international Internet traffic subjected to Deep Packet Inspection (DPI) or other higher levels of scrutiny that would slow the flow of the traffic. As a last resort, failure to improve could result in the blacklisting of national IP ranges of the worst offender nations by the organization's member states.[18]

### TIE INTERNET INFRASTRUCTURE DEVELOPMENT AID TO CYBERSECURITY COOPERATION

The new organization should also work with other international organizations that promote the development of Internet infrastructure to ensure that these investments are carried out in conjunction with investments in the development of legal, incident-response, and enforcement capabilities. This effort can also be promoted within the U.S. government. Projects by the United States Agency for International Development (USAID) to lay fiber in developing countries should be done in concert with legal assistance from the Justice Department in developing investigation and prosecutorial capabilities. Currently, there is no connection between the two efforts. The State Department should also pressure allied nations and international development organizations to adopt similar policies.

### ESTABLISH OPERATIONS CENTERS TO COORDINATE REQUESTS FOR ASSISTANCE

Finally, the organization could help resolve the problem of international coordination to stop cyber crimes in progress and to investigate and prosecute attacks that cross international boundaries once they have occurred. The current bilateral process is slow, cumbersome, and expensive, even for the United States with its well-staffed embassies and legal attaché offices spread across the globe, let alone for smaller states that often fall victim to cyber crime. The Group of Eight (G8) Subgroup on High-Tech Crime has laid the groundwork for this effort, providing a mechanism for cooperating on cyber crime on a 24/7 basis. This effort could be improved upon by having the organization establish operations centers around the globe staffed by member country law enforcement personnel. These centers could provide a twenty-four-hour resource, providing a valuable link between law enforcement personnel and network security operations centers. One goal of this effort should be to create a mechanism by which requests from government agencies and the private sector in one country can be passed to authorities in another country and then passed down to network operators to have command-and-control servers or hosts in botnets shut down.

# *LIMITING STATE ACTION IN CYBERSPACE*

Cyber crime is only a part of the current security deficiency in cyberspace. State activity may be doing more to undermine trust in the network than cyber criminals. Whereas cyber crime can be written off as a cost of doing business, the actions of state actors threaten the very model of connectivity and the resultant efficiency gains. Because state actors present an altogether higher level of capability, nothing that is connected to the network can be considered beyond their reach. As a result, if state actors cannot be constrained through technical defenses, they must be constrained in other ways. If constraints cannot be put into place, the efficiency gains from connecting to the network may end up costing more than they are worth. If critical infrastructure continues to be routinely exploited, preparation of the battlefield may by itself create conflicts where none would have existed. If states continue to target foreign companies' intellectual property and to transfer that intellectual property to national companies, the global system of research and development that allows around-the-clock work to be conducted may be dismantled.

## *END OPPOSITION TO TALKS*
## *ON WARFARE AND ESPIONAGE IN CYBERSPACE*

To address these concerns, the United States must work to develop new norms of state behavior in cyberspace. For the past decade, the United States has stood in opposition to any discussions on these areas and attempted to keep the international community focused only on addressing cyber crime. U.S. opposition stems from a view that commitments by states to restrict their activities in cyberspace would not be honored and that verification that states are meeting their commitments would be all but impossible.[19] This position, however, is derived from the application of the Cold War arms control experience, which is not readily applicable to the current problem of cybersecurity. Limited and focused international agreements could benefit the United States in some cases. Moreover, U.S. unwillingness to engage in negotiations on this subject only lends credence to the view that the United States seeks hegemonic domination of cyberspace.

The United States is the most feared bogeyman in cyberspace, given its historical role in developing the underlying technologies and the high level of capability within U.S. military and intelligence agencies. Maintaining U.S. capabilities in exploitation and attack at a level above all rivals is certainly in U.S. interests; being perceived as having and using these capabilities clearly is not. The militarization of cyberspace threatens the single, global, interoperable network, the existence of which has created tremendous economic growth, tied nations more closely together through shared commerce, and accelerated the exchange of ideas across cultural and international boundaries. Refusing to engage publicly in negotiations over limiting cyber warfare only increases fears that the United States seeks to dominate cyberspace and plans to use the domain to gain war-fighting advantage. The United States should make every effort to offset that perception. Negotiations may not lead to the creation of a treaty, but there is little harm in entering into them. The Obama administration has embraced the value of talking internationally. Cyber warfare should be no exception. Participation in the UN Group of Governmental Experts by the United States is a good start but engagement must be far wider and deeper.

Engagement does not mean, however, that the United States is forced to accept current treaty options that are not in U.S. interests. The current Russian proposal for arms control in cyberspace would commit signatories to abstain from developing offensive cyber capabilities or from engaging in cyber espionage, while providing no viable mechanisms for verification. The historical record of the chemical and biological weapons conventions raises doubts as to whether treaty commitments that cannot be verified will lead to meaningful reductions. Moreover, if the United States met its obligations but other signatories did not, a treaty without verification would place the United States at a strategic disadvantage.

The focus on restricting the development of cyber weapons conveys a lack of understanding of the true nature of cyber warfare. Advanced threats in cyberspace are not automated bots or worms, but human actors. The most potent weapons are not logic bombs and Trojan horses but the people who design them and can use them as part of an organized, persistent effort to gain access to targeted systems, exploit them for information advantage, and corrupt or destroy data. Moreover, any defensive program requires mastery of offensive operations to be able to defend against those operations. In cyber warfare, the ability to replicate a software program instantly means that any exploits developed for the purposes of testing countermeasures can quickly be turned into an offensive operation. Given this reality, attempts to limit the development of offensive cyber operations will come to naught because verification that states had not developed such capabilities would be all but impossible.

### EXAMINE TREATY OPTIONS AND NORMS DEVELOPMENT AGAINST TARGETING CIVILIAN SYSTEMS

The problem of verification, however, does not mean that there are no issues that international negotiations and agreements could meaningfully address. Instead of focusing on limiting the development of cyber weapons, treaty efforts should focus on limiting state actor penetration into civilian systems that have limited, if any, intelligence value. Currently, too many countries are conducting offensive cyber operations under the separate but related guises of "espionage" and "preparation of the battlefield." Actions such as penetrating the power grids of foreign nations so that they can be taken down in a time of war are destabilizing and increase the likelihood that a conflict in cyberspace will spill over into the physical world. The United States should also seek to avoid having cyberattacks turn into a new and dangerous form of protest, somewhere between issuing a demarche and a military response. If cyberattacks become an acceptable form of international protest, the effects could be extremely destabilizing economically and could open the door to conventional military conflict.

International agreements to set power grids, the financial sector, and other components of civilian infrastructure off limits may ultimately be in U.S. interests. But at this stage, most countries, including the United States, are likely unwilling to foreswear the intelligence value gained from exploiting these systems. The U.S. government should begin a process to determine whether and under what conditions such agreements would be in U.S. interests (the fragility of these systems and the costs associated with protecting them may ultimately outweigh the benefits gained in exploiting adversary systems). Though it may be too early for such a proposal to meet with adequate support within the U.S. government and foreign governments, two areas are already ripe for an international agreement to limit state action in cyberspace. In each area, there are no intelligence interests at stake. The United States should develop proposals to address separately the security and sanctity of root operations that allow the Internet to function and to ban denial-of-service attacks.

## *RECOGNIZE THE ROOT AS A STRATEGIC*
## *INTERNATIONAL ASSET*

The root has been at the core of Internet governance since the development of the Domain Name System in the 1980s. DNS provides the necessary link between human-readable domain names like CFR.org and machine-readable IP addresses like 66.40.21.148. The DNS relies on thirteen root servers to provide authoritative information for all top-level domains (.com, .net, .us, .jp, etc.) to begin the process of resolving a request for a webpage or email server. Efforts are under way to improve the security of the root, but root operations remain vulnerable to both penetration attempts and large-scale, distributed, denial-of-service attacks. Because the information contained in the root zone file is by its nature public, no intelligence value can be gained from attempting to gain access to a root server. An agreement to recognize the root as an international strategic asset that states will not attempt to disrupt would be in U.S. interests and could serve as a first step to reducing tensions in cyberspace. U.S. control of the root continues to be an issue, and while the United States has wished to maintain this role only to ensure that the root continues to function, it may be in U.S. interests to find an international mechanism for stewardship of the root as part of a grand bargain on Internet governance.

## *PURSUE A TREATY TO BAN DENIAL-OF-SERVICE ATTACKS*

As with a treaty to protect the root, an international agreement to ban denial-of-service attacks would focus on a narrow problem that is not complicated by intelligence collection. Denial-of-service attacks are, by their nature, brute-force weapons that do not require networks to be penetrated, but only disrupted. They are also a devastating weapon that has been employed both criminally and in state-level conflict. In at least three instances, the Russian government and military have engaged in or encouraged denial-of-service attacks on foreign nations that crippled the victims' Internet infrastructure and the services that relied on it. These attacks include the 2007 attack targeting Estonia, the 2008 attack targeting Georgia, and the 2009 attack targeting Kyrgyzstan. Unlike computer network exploitation, which may be used for sabotage or espionage, denial-of-service attacks can only serve the purpose of sabotaging a system. Thus, the United States should promote a treaty that would commit signatories to a policy of limiting denial-of-service attacks outside conventional conflicts. Banning such attacks under an international treaty could be the first step to establishing responsibility in cyberspace. Most denial-of-service attacks are carried out by criminals for the purpose of extortion. The assistance that states provide in shutting down a distributed denial-of-service attack can be used to judge whether the attack is condoned by the state or conducted against its will. If states assist in stopping the attack, then the attack should be treated as a criminal matter. On the other hand, if states are not responsive, it should be taken to signify official approval of the attack and therefore viewed as a hostile act.

## LAYING OUT THE TECHNICAL AGENDA

To date, the focus of the Internet technical community has been on interoperability. As the technologies that make the Internet work continue to evolve, that focus needs to shift to security. The Internet's underlying technologies were designed for a closed network in which access was closely controlled and all users were trusted. They were not built and designed for the purposes for which they are now being used. This problem, long recognized within technical circles, has yet to be adequately addressed. The 2003 *U.S. National Strategy to Secure Cyberspace* identified vulnerabilities within three "key Internet protocols": the Internet Protocol, which guides data from source to destination across the Internet; the Domain Name System, which translates IP numbers into recognizable Web addresses; and the Border Gateway Protocol, which provides the connection between networks to create the "network of networks."[20] None of these protocols has built-in mechanisms to verify the origin or authenticity of information sent to them, leaving them vulnerable to being spoofed or otherwise manipulated by malicious actors. The 2003 strategy recognized these problems but concluded that "private industry is leading the effort to ensure that the core functions of the Internet develop in a secure manner" and limited the role of the federal government to coordinating "public-private partnerships to encourage . . . the adoption of improved security protocols."[21] Nearly a decade later, these problems still plague the Internet.

At this point, it is safe to conclude that the "coordination" and "encouragement" model has not yielded the desired results, and stronger leadership by the federal government is necessary.

By providing leadership, technical assistance, and funding, the United States can foster the development and adoption of a new set of secure protocols that will address many of the vulnerabilities in the current Internet architecture yet forestall the development and adoption of protocols that go too far toward the development of an online surveillance state or risk the breakup of the Internet into a series of Balkanized and unconnected national networks. As Marcus Sachs has written, the goal is to avoid a "technical Cold War" in which the United States, China, and Europe develop "technically different and noninteroperable computer networks based on protocols and rules that fit each society's values, ethics, and legal systems."[22]

## DIRECT THE NATIONAL SCIENCE FOUNDATION TO DEVELOP A TECHNICAL CHALLENGE TO THE IETF TO DEVELOP SECURE PROTOCOLS

The best way to forestall this outcome is to help create a suite of protocols that adequately addresses security concerns without breaking up the Internet or turning it into a global platform for state control. For more than two decades, the Internet Engineering Task Force has driven the development of the technical standards that make the Internet function. An open community of technical experts from around the world, the IETF and its members have guided the evolution of the Internet for a generation and should be given the opportunity to address the security deficiencies that plague the current network. In concert with its allies, the U.S. government should challenge the IETF to develop a new suite of more secure protocols. The goal, best stated by former director of national intelligence John Michael "Mike" McConnell, should be to "reengineer the Internet to make attribution, geolocation, intelligence analysis and impact assessment—who did it, from where, why and what was the result—more manageable."[23] It should not, however, seek to embed into the underlying code of the Internet perfect attribution that would be the ultimate tool of the surveillance state.

The National Science Foundation (NSF) should lead the effort to develop the technical challenge and should do so in consultation with relevant federal agencies, the private sector, and academic institutions.

The initial phase should focus on clearly stating the problems caused by a lack of security on the Internet and then identify whether and how these problems can be addressed through the development of new technical standards. The NSF should then issue the challenge and oversee a system of grants issued through the IETF. The challenge should include a deadline of four years to present a suite of secure protocols and begin implementing them. In presenting this challenge, it should be made clear that failure to meet the deadline would result in the initiation of a federal effort to create new protocols. The United States should fund this activity, seeking support from other states that agree with the approach as articulated, to ensure that the challenge is met and that the protocols developed align with overall U.S. objectives for developing cyberspace. Then, incentives must be provided to promote their implementation.

# Organizing the U.S. Effort

Cyber Command is busy working to fuse the cyber units of the U.S. Army, Navy, Air Force, and Marines into a coordinated effort to protect Defense Department networks; support ground, sea, and air missions; and conduct offensive operations in cyberspace when directed. Legislation being considered in the Senate would give the Department of Homeland Security the mission of securing all civilian government systems and additional power to regulate critical infrastructure in the private sector for cybersecurity. A parallel effort is necessary to ensure that diplomatic efforts with foreign states and within Internet governance forums are coordinated, resourced, and in pursuit of defined U.S. objectives.

## APPOINT A DEPUTY WHITE HOUSE CYBERSECURITY COORDINATOR FOR INTERNET GOVERNANCE

In the Clinton administration, a single official, Ira Magaziner, effectively managed the establishment of Internet governance policy and engagement with Internet governance forums. The issue is now too broad for one person to manage effectively, but the White House must have a lead on Internet governance to coordinate the development of policy and oversee its implementation. The legislation that would broaden the Department of Homeland Security's power would also establish within the Executive Office of the President the Office of Cyberspace Policy, moving it into the existing cybersecurity coordinator role and strengthening the position's authority, budget, and staffing. The director of this office should be given a deputy for coordinating U.S. Internet governance policy with a staff to perform oversight, ensuring that the U.S. agenda in cyberspace is being promoted at every opportunity.

## CREATE A NEW BUREAU OF CYBER AFFAIRS
## WITHIN THE STATE DEPARTMENT

The State Department should be reorganized and staffed to pursue the U.S. agenda in cyberspace, placing the requisite focus on securing the domain in all forums and bilateral relations where cyberspace comes into play. Although the State Department is currently overly focused on the issue of Internet freedom to the detriment of cybersecurity, that bias can be corrected by giving the department a clear mission for Internet governance that brings these seemingly competing interests into balance and by adequately and appropriately staffing the organization with requisite expertise and experience. At a minimum, the State Department should have the resources to coordinate positions across the government and accompany all delegations. Full-time positions or State Department liaisons should also be created at other relevant agencies. The investment required is comparatively miniscule, but the benefits would be enormous.

Following the confirmation of General Keith Alexander to head Cyber Command and his promotion to four-star general, the Defense Department's efforts in cyberspace are led by the fifteenth-highest-ranking official in the department. With the creation of Cyber Command within the Defense Department, an equal level of importance should be given to the issue of cyber diplomacy at the State Department. To do that, Congress should create a Bureau of Cyber Affairs under the State Department's undersecretary for political affairs. Organizations within the State Department currently responsible for international telecommunications issues, Internet freedom, and cybersecurity should be brought into this new bureau. These include the Office of Cyber Affairs in Intelligence and Research, which is responsible for analysis of cybersecurity issues, interagency coordination, and international affairs; the International Communication and Information Policy group within the Bureau of Economic, Energy, and Business Affairs; and the Global Internet Freedom Task Force.

## CREATE A CENTRALIZED FORUM FOR THE PRIVATE
## SECTOR TO COORDINATE INTERNET GOVERNANCE
## AGENDAS WITH THE U.S. GOVERNMENT

The new Bureau of Cyber Affairs should also bring under it existing advisory committees within the State Department related to information technology, including the Advisory Committee on International

Communications and Information Policy and the International Tele-communication Advisory Committee. In addition, a new commit-tee should be established that is singularly focused on cybersecurity. A single office serving these committees should provide a centralized forum for the private sector to coordinate Internet governance agendas with the U.S. government. U.S. companies like Microsoft and Syman-tec are important players in Internet governance forums. At present, they are shouldering too much of the burden and lack clear direction on how to promote U.S. national interests. Though U.S. companies may not always be aligned with the position of the government, they should have the opportunity to shape that position and to understand the agenda that the U.S. government is advocating.

### INCREASE FUNDING FOR ENGAGEMENT WITH INTERNET GOVERNANCE FORUMS

The appointment of a senior White House official for Internet gover-nance and the creation of a new bureau within the State Department to manage this issue does not mean that other agencies do not have inter-ests or should not have a role in international engagement on Internet governance. To the contrary, the departments of Defense, Commerce, Justice, and Homeland Security—as well as subdepartment entities such as the National Telecommunications and Information Adminis-tration and the FBI—will continue to have active multilateral and bilat-eral partnerships, but will do so within a construct that promotes the overall U.S. agenda. Their international affairs offices or those entities engaged in Internet governance forums should be appropriately staffed at a sufficiently senior level and given the time and resources to prepare to engage. Currently, Internet governance is not anyone's day job.

# Conclusion

The Internet is at a crucial point in its relatively early history. Malicious activity carried out by criminals, spies, and war fighters threaten the economic growth and efficiency that the existence of a single, global interoperable network has brought. If these threats are not addressed constructively through wider U.S. engagement, other countries will step in and may architect a solution that would deprive the Internet of the very characteristics that have made it valuable in the first place.

Given these factors, the United States should move beyond its traditional opposition to engagement on issues of Internet governance and lead efforts among like-minded countries to address security concerns in ways that will enhance rather than detract from the Internet as an engine of economic growth. The United States must work to develop new international mechanisms to stop cyberattacks, pursue cyber criminals, and rein in state actors engaged in malicious activity. Together with investments to rearchitect the Internet's underlying protocols to make them more secure, these efforts can preserve and extend the economic value derived from the Internet.

# Endnotes

1. "Unsecured Economies: Protecting Vital Information," McAfee, January 21, 2009, http://www.mcafee.com/us/about/press/corporate/2009/20090129_063500_j.html.
2. *Virtually Here: The Age of Cyber Warfare*, McAfee Virtual Criminology Report, 2009, p. 13.
3. Joshua Davis, "Hackers Take Down the Most Wired Country in Europe," *Wired*, October 21, 2007.
4. Stewart Baker, Shaun Waterman, and George Ivanov, *In the Crossfire: Critical Infrastructure in the Age of Cyber War* (Santa Clara, CA: McAfee, 2010).
5. As defined in federal law, the term *Internet* means the international computer network of both federal and nonfederal interoperable packet switched data networks.
6. Jeremy Malcolm, *Multi-stakeholder Governance and the Internet Governance Forum* (Perth: Terminus Press, 2008), p. 32.
7. "Salvador Declaration Calls for Criminal Justice Reform to Safeguard Human Rights, Security and Development," UN Office on Drugs and Crime, April 19, 2010, http://www.unodc.org/southerncone/en/frontpage/2010/04/19-declaracao-de-salvador-pede-uma-reforma-da-justica-criminal-para-proteger-os-direitos-humanos-a-seguranca-e-o-desenvolvimento.html.
8. UN System Chief Executives Board for Coordination, First Regular Session of 2010, UNIDO Headquarters, Vienna, April 9, 2010, pp. 11–12.
9. "Connecting America: The National Broadband Plan," Federal Communications Commission, March 15, 2010, p. xi, http://download.broadband.gov/plan/national-broadband-plan.pdf.
10. For an in-depth discussion of this issue, see Robert K. Knake, "Untangling Attribution: Moving to Accountability in Cyberspace," testimony before the House of Representatives Committee on Science and Technology, July 15, 2010, http://www.cfr.org/publication/22630/untangling_attribution.html.
11. Jason Healey at the Cyber Conflict Studies Association developed this concept in "Beyond Attribution: A Vocabulary for National Responsibility for Cyber Attacks," April 1, 2010, http://www.cyberconflict.org/ccsa-in-the-news/jasonhealeyslatestpaper.
12. "Cybercrime Convention: A Positive Beginning to a Long Road Ahead," *Journal of High Technology Law*, vol. 2, no. 1, 2003, p. 110.
13. Council of Europe, "Convention on Cybercrime," CETS No. 185, July 1, 2004, http://conventions.coe.int/Treaty/Commun/QueVoulezVous.asp?NT=185&CL=ENG.
14. Financial Action Task Force, "About the Financial Action Task Force," http://www.fatf-gafi.org/pages/0,3417,en_32250379_32236836_1_1_1_1_1,00.html.
15. For an overview of FATF, see "An Introduction to FATF and Its Work," FATF-GAFI, 2010, http://www.fatf-gafi.org/dataoecd/48/11/45139480.pdf.
16. For more information on the ITU Toolkit for Cybercrime Legislation, see "ITU Cybercrime Legislation Resources: ITU Toolkit for Cybercrime Legislation," International

Telecommunications Union, http://www.itu.int/ITU-D/cyb/cybersecurity/projects/
cyberlaw.html.

17. Oxford Internet Institute, "Mapping and Measuring Cybercrime (Invited Forum),"
University of Oxford, January 22, 2010, http://www.oii.ox.ac.uk/events/?id=337.

18. A unilateral approach is being contemplated in the U.S. Senate. The International
Cyber Crime Reporting and Cooperation Act would require the president to provide
an annual assessment on international cyber crime and to suspend aid, financing, and
trade programs based on the findings. Cosponsored by senators Kirsten Gillibrand
(D-NY) and Orrin Hatch (R-UT), the bill has its merits, but fails in one important
aspect. The bill would not assess one of the biggest cyber criminal sanctuaries—the
United States—decreasing the likelihood that it will have the desired shaming effect.
Moreover, any sanctions instituted by the United States based on these rankings are
not likely to have the desired effect on target countries of improving behavior.

19. See Richard Clarke and Robert K. Knake, *Cyber War: The Next Threat to National Security and What to Do About It* (New York: HarperCollins, 2010).

20. The White House, *The National Strategy to Secure Cyberspace*, February 2003, p. 30.

21. Ibid.

22. Marcus H. Sachs, *Who e-Governs?* George Mason University, Policy Analysis Research Paper, December 4, 2007, p. 14.

23. "Mike McConnell on How to Win the Cyber War We're Losing," *Washington Post*,
February 28, 2010.

# About the Author

**Robert K. Knake** is an international affairs fellow in residence at the Council on Foreign Relations studying cyber war. Prior to his fellowship, he was a principal at Good Harbor Consulting, LLC, a security strategy consulting firm with offices in Washington, DC; Boston; and Abu Dhabi, where he served domestic and foreign clients on cybersecurity and homeland security projects.

During the 2008 presidential campaign, Knake coordinated the Counterterrorism Task Force for the Obama campaign and served on the Homeland Security Task Force. Following the election of President Barack Obama, Knake served on the presidential transition team at the U.S. Department of Homeland Security and authored the agency review team's final report.

Knake joined Good Harbor after earning his MA from Harvard University's Kennedy School of Government. He has been quoted widely as an expert on cybersecurity and has appeared as a speaker or panelist at numerous events on cybersecurity, including DEFCON and the annual meeting of the American Bar Association. In July 2010, he testified before Congress on the role of attribution in deterring cyberattacks. In 2006, Knake and CFR Senior Fellow Steven Simon directed the Century Foundation Task Force report, *The Forgotten Homeland*. Knake is coauthor (with former chair of the U.S. Counterterrorism Security Group Richard A. Clarke) of *Cyber War: The Next Threat to National Security and What to Do About It*.

# Advisory Committee
## for *Internet Governance in an Age of Cyber Insecurity*

Marvin Ammori
*University of Nebraska College of Law*

Stanley S. Arkin
*The Arkin Group, LLC*

Stewart A. Baker
*Steptoe & Johnson LLP*

Daniel F. Burton Jr.
*Salesforce.com*

Michael R. Cote
*SecureWorks*

James P. Dougherty, *ex officio*
*Council on Foreign Relations*

Esther Dyson
*EDventure Holdings, Inc.*

Clark Kent Ervin
*The Aspen Institute*

Michael Hayden
*Chertoff Group*

Jason Healey
*Cyber Conflict Studies Association*

Jamie Hedlund
*Internet Corporation for Assigned Names and Numbers*

Jessica R. Herrera-Flanigan
*Monument Policy Group, LLC*

Tiffany Jones
*Symantec Corporation*

Catherine B. Lotrionte
*Georgetown University*

Bruce W. MacDonald
*U.S. Strategic Posture Review Commission*

Charles J. McLaughlin
*Accenture*

James C. Mulvenon
*Center for Intelligence Research and Analysis*

Stewart M. Patrick, *ex officio*
*Council on Foreign Relations*

Michael N. Pocalyko
*Monticello Capital LLC*

Daniel B. Prieto III
*IBM Corporation*

Greg Rattray
*Delta Risk, LLC*

Harvey Rishikof
*The National War College*

Eric Rosenbach
*Belfer Center for Science & International Affairs*

Marcus H. Sachs
*Verizon Communications Inc.*

John M. Scott
*Mercury Federal Systems*

Adam Segal, *ex officio*
*Council on Foreign Relations*

Wes Spain
*Lawrence Livermore National Laboratory*

Suzanne Spaulding
*Bingham McCutchen LLP*

Frederick S. Tipson
*United Nations Development Program*

Frances Townsend
*Baker Botts, LLP*

Herbert S. Winokur Jr.
*Capricorn Holdings, Inc.*

John Woods
*Hunton & Williams, LLP*

Amit Yoran
*NetWitness*

Lee Zeichner
*Zeichner Risk Analytics, LLC*

# Mission Statement
## of the International Institutions and Global Governance Program

The International Institutions and Global Governance (IIGG) program at CFR aims to identify the institutional requirements for effective multilateral cooperation in the twenty-first century. The program is motivated by recognition that the architecture of global governance—largely reflecting the world as it existed in 1945—has not kept pace with fundamental changes in the international system. These shifts include the spread of transnational challenges, the rise of new powers, and the mounting influence of nonstate actors. Existing multilateral arrangements thus provide an inadequate foundation for addressing many of today's most pressing threats and opportunities and for advancing U.S. national and broader global interests.

Given these trends, U.S. policymakers and other interested actors require rigorous, independent analysis of current structures of multilateral cooperation, and of the promises and pitfalls of alternative institutional arrangements. The IIGG program meets these needs by analyzing the strengths and weaknesses of existing multilateral institutions and proposing reforms tailored to new international circumstances.

The IIGG program fulfills its mandate by

- Engaging CFR fellows in research on improving existing and building new frameworks to address specific global challenges—including climate change, the proliferation of weapons of mass destruction, transnational terrorism, and global health—and disseminating the research through books, articles, Council Special Reports, and other outlets;

- Bringing together influential foreign policymakers, scholars, and CFR members to debate the merits of international regimes and frameworks at meetings in New York, Washington, DC, and other select cities;

– Hosting roundtable series whose objectives are to inform the foreign policy community of today's international governance challenges and breed inventive solutions to strengthen the world's multilateral bodies; and

– Providing a state-of-the-art Web presence as a resource to the wider foreign policy community on issues related to the future of global governance.

# Council Special Reports

*Published by the Council on Foreign Relations*

*From Rome to Kampala: The U.S. Approach to the 2010 International Criminal Court Review Conference*
Vijay Padmanabhan; CSR No. 55, April 2010

*Strengthening the Nuclear Nonproliferation Regime*
Paul Lettow; CSR No. 54, April 2010
An International Institutions and Global Governance Program Report

*The Russian Economic Crisis*
Jeffrey Mankoff; CSR No. 53, April 2010

*Somalia: A New Approach*
Bronwyn E. Bruton; CSR No. 52, March 2010
A Center for Preventive Action Report

*The Future of NATO*
James M. Goldgeier; CSR No. 51, February 2010
An International Institutions and Global Governance Program Report

*The United States in the New Asia*
Evan A. Feigenbaum and Robert A. Manning; CSR No. 50, November 2009
An International Institutions and Global Governance Program Report

*Intervention to Stop Genocide and Mass Atrocities: International Norms and U.S. Policy*
Matthew C. Waxman; CSR No. 49, October 2009
An International Institutions and Global Governance Program Report

*Enhancing U.S. Preventive Action*
Paul B. Stares and Micah Zenko; CSR No. 48, October 2009
A Center for Preventive Action Report

*The Canadian Oil Sands: Energy Security vs. Climate Change*
Michael A. Levi; CSR No. 47, May 2009
A Maurice R. Greenberg Center for Geoeconomic Studies Report

*The National Interest and the Law of the Sea*
Scott G. Borgerson; CSR No. 46, May 2009

*Lessons of the Financial Crisis*
Benn Steil; CSR No. 45, March 2009
A Maurice R. Greenberg Center for Geoeconomic Studies Report

*Global Imbalances and the Financial Crisis*
Steven Dunaway; CSR No. 44, March 2009
A Maurice R. Greenberg Center for Geoeconomic Studies Report

*Eurasian Energy Security*
Jeffrey Mankoff; CSR No. 43, February 2009

*Preparing for Sudden Change in North Korea*
Paul B. Stares and Joel S. Wit; CSR No. 42, January 2009
A Center for Preventive Action Report

*Averting Crisis in Ukraine*
Steven Pifer; CSR No. 41, January 2009
A Center for Preventive Action Report

*Congo: Securing Peace, Sustaining Progress*
Anthony W. Gambino; CSR No. 40, October 2008
A Center for Preventive Action Report

*Deterring State Sponsorship of Nuclear Terrorism*
Michael A. Levi; CSR No. 39, September 2008

*China, Space Weapons, and U.S. Security*
Bruce W. MacDonald; CSR No. 38, September 2008

*Sovereign Wealth and Sovereign Power: The Strategic Consequences of American Indebtedness*
Brad W. Setser; CSR No. 37, September 2008
A Maurice R. Greenberg Center for Geoeconomic Studies Report

*Securing Pakistan's Tribal Belt*
Daniel Markey; CSR No. 36, July 2008 (Web-only release) and August 2008
A Center for Preventive Action Report

*Avoiding Transfers to Torture*
Ashley S. Deeks; CSR No. 35, June 2008

*Global FDI Policy: Correcting a Protectionist Drift*
David M. Marchick and Matthew J. Slaughter; CSR No. 34, June 2008
A Maurice R. Greenberg Center for Geoeconomic Studies Report

*Dealing with Damascus: Seeking a Greater Return on U.S.-Syria Relations*
Mona Yacoubian and Scott Lasensky; CSR No. 33, June 2008
A Center for Preventive Action Report

*Climate Change and National Security: An Agenda for Action*
Joshua W. Busby; CSR No. 32, November 2007
A Maurice R. Greenberg Center for Geoeconomic Studies Report

*Planning for Post-Mugabe Zimbabwe*
Michelle D. Gavin; CSR No. 31, October 2007
A Center for Preventive Action Report

*U.S.-India Nuclear Cooperation: A Strategy for Moving Forward*
Michael A. Levi and Charles D. Ferguson; CSR No. 16, June 2006

*Generating Momentum for a New Era in U.S.-Turkey Relations*
Steven A. Cook and Elizabeth Sherwood-Randall; CSR No. 15, June 2006

*Peace in Papua: Widening a Window of Opportunity*
Blair A. King; CSR No. 14, March 2006
A Center for Preventive Action Report

*Neglected Defense: Mobilizing the Private Sector to Support Homeland Security*
Stephen E. Flynn and Daniel B. Prieto; CSR No. 13, March 2006

*Afghanistan's Uncertain Transition From Turmoil to Normalcy*
Barnett R. Rubin; CSR No. 12, March 2006
A Center for Preventive Action Report

*Preventing Catastrophic Nuclear Terrorism*
Charles D. Ferguson; CSR No. 11, March 2006

*Getting Serious About the Twin Deficits*
Menzie D. Chinn; CSR No. 10, September 2005
A Maurice R. Greenberg Center for Geoeconomic Studies Report

*Both Sides of the Aisle: A Call for Bipartisan Foreign Policy*
Nancy E. Roman; CSR No. 9, September 2005

*Forgotten Intervention? What the United States Needs to Do in the Western Balkans*
Amelia Branczik and William L. Nash; CSR No. 8, June 2005
A Center for Preventive Action Report

*A New Beginning: Strategies for a More Fruitful Dialogue with the Muslim World*
Craig Charney and Nicole Yakatan; CSR No. 7, May 2005

*Power-Sharing in Iraq*
David L. Phillips; CSR No. 6, April 2005
A Center for Preventive Action Report

*Giving Meaning to "Never Again": Seeking an Effective Response to the Crisis
in Darfur and Beyond*
Cheryl O. Igiri and Princeton N. Lyman; CSR No. 5, September 2004

*Freedom, Prosperity, and Security: The G8 Partnership with Africa: Sea Island 2004 and Beyond*
J. Brian Atwood, Robert S. Browne, and Princeton N. Lyman; CSR No. 4, May 2004

*Addressing the HIV/AIDS Pandemic: A U.S. Global AIDS Strategy for the Long Term*
Daniel M. Fox and Princeton N. Lyman; CSR No. 3, May 2004
Cosponsored with the Milbank Memorial Fund

*Challenges for a Post-Election Philippines*
Catharin E. Dalpino; CSR No. 2, May 2004
A Center for Preventive Action Report

*Stability, Security, and Sovereignty in the Republic of Georgia*
David L. Phillips; CSR No. 1, January 2004
A Center for Preventive Action Report

To purchase a printed copy, call the Brookings Institution Press: 800.537.5487.
*Note:* Council Special Reports are available for download from CFR's website, www.cfr.org.
For more information, email publications@cfr.org.